S0-BNJ-716

U.S. Symbols

by Ann-Marie Kishel

first step nonfiction

Lerner Publications Company · Minneapolis

What makes you think of the United States of America?

A U.S. **symbol** makes you think of America.

There are many symbols of
the United States.

You might think of the
U.S. flag.

We say the Pledge of
Allegiance to the flag.

We promise to **respect** the United States.

We sing the national **anthem**.

Our national anthem is called "The Star-Spangled Banner."

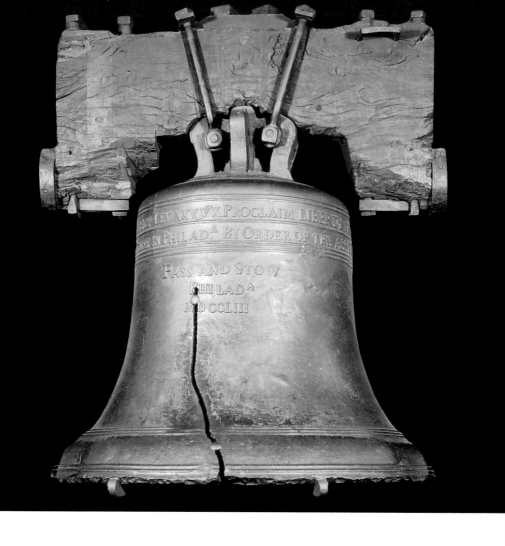

The Liberty Bell is in Philadelphia.

It rang when the United
States became a country.

The Statue of Liberty is in New York.

People think of freedom
when they see it.

The bald eagle is our national bird.

It **represents** freedom,
strength, and courage.

These are all symbols of the United States.

What U.S. symbols do you see around you?

Flying the Flag at Half-Mast

A flag is sometimes flown at half-mast (also called half-staff). This means it is only raised halfway up the flag pole.

The president or a governor decides when the flag will be flown at half-mast. The flag is flown at half-mast when an important person dies or when many people die.

U.S. Symbols Facts

 Francis Scott Key wrote "The Star-Spangled Banner" in 1814.

 The Liberty Bell has a large crack in it. It can no longer be rung. It was rung for the last time on February 26, 1846, for George Washington's birthday.

 The Statue of Liberty was given to the people of the United States by the people of France.

The United States Postal Service uses the bald eagle as its symbol.

 The bald eagle is only found in North America.

 Benjamin Franklin thought the national bird should be the turkey instead of the bald eagle.

Glossary

 anthem – a song that expresses patriotism

 represents – stands for or means something else

 respect – to honor

 symbol – something that stands for or means something else

Index

Copyright © 2007 by Lerner Publishing Group, Inc.

All rights reserved. International copyright secured. No part of this book may be reproduced, stored in a retrieval system, or transmitted in any form or by any means—electronic, mechanical, photocopying, recording, or otherwise—without the prior written permission of Lerner Publishing Group, Inc., except for the inclusion of brief quotations in an acknowledged review.

The photographs in this book are reproduced with the permission of: PhotoDisc Royalty Free by Getty Images, front cover, pp. 2, 12, 14, 16 (upper right, lower right), 22 (second from top); © Chip Somodevilla/Getty Images, pp. 3, 22 (bottom); © Don Murray/Getty Images, p. 4; © Royalty-Free/Corbis, pp. 5, 16 (upper left); © Stephen Jaffe/AFP/Getty Images, p. 6; © William Thomas Cain/Getty Images, pp. 7, 22 (second from bottom); © Elsa/Getty Images, p. 8, 22 (top); © Jamie Squire/Getty Images, p. 9; © SuperStock, pp. 10, 16 (lower left); Library of Congress (LC-USZC2-729), p. 11; © Brian Snyder/Reuters/CORBIS, p. 13; © Todd Strand/Independent Picture Service, pp. 15, 17; © Mike Theiler/Getty Images, p. 18.

Lerner Publishing Company
A division of Lerner Publishing Group, Inc.
241 First Avenue North
Minneapolis, MN 55401 U.S.A.

Website address: www.lernerbooks.com

Library of Congress Cataloging-in-Publication Data

Kishel, Ann-Marie.
    U.S. symbols / by Ann-Marie Kishel.
        p.   cm. — (First step nonfiction)
    Includes index.
    ISBN-13: 978–0–8225–6394–5 (lib. bdg. : alk. paper)
    ISBN-10: 0–8225–6394–0 (lib. bdg. : alk. paper)
    1. Signs and symbols—United States—Juvenile literature. 2. Patriotism—United States—
Juvenile literature. I. Title. II. Title: United States symbols.
E156.K58 2007
929.90973—dc22   2006018518

Manufactured in the United States of America
2 – DP – 7/1/11